MO
FARAH

Roy Apps

Illustrated by Chris King

LONDON•SYDNEY

First published in 2013 by
Franklin Watts
338 Euston Road
London NW1 3BH

Franklin Watts Australia
Level 17/207 Kent Street
Sydney NSW 2000

Text © Roy Apps 2013
Illustrations © Chris King 2013
Cover design by Peter Scoulding

A CIP catalogue record for this book
is available from the British Library.

ISBN: 978 1 4451 1833 8

7

Printed in Great Britain

Franklin Watts is a division of Hachette Children's Books,
an Hachette UK company.
www.hachette.co.uk

Chapter One:

Twin Brothers And Best Of Friends

The two oldest boys had elected themselves captains of the two football teams and were choosing who they wanted on their sides.

"I'll have Mo and Hassan," said the first boy.

"That's not fair!" protested the other boy. "If you have both Mo and Hassan, we won't stand a chance!"

This was true. Mo and his identical twin brother Hassan were the best footballers on the street. They were only eight years old, but they were both tall and quick on their feet.

"OK," said the first boy, "I'll have Mo and you can pick Hassan."

The game of football was fast and furious. Mo skipped over a couple of opposition players and found himself in front of their goal. Suddenly, Hassan barged into him and knocked him flying. If there had been a referee, he would definitely have given a penalty. Mo got to his feet and started shoving his twin brother. Hassan shoved him back. Then they both burst out laughing. As well as being twin brothers, they were the best of friends.

They rejoined the game of football. This time it was Hassan's turn to make

a dizzying run on the opposition's goal.
Behind them, a few blocks away, came
the sound of traffic on one of Djibouti's
main highways. A little further away,
across the border, came the familiar
rasp of guns being fired. Somalia, a
neighbouring country, was at war; a
war that was getting fiercer and more
dangerous with every passing day.

Chapter Two:

The Parting

Mo and Hassan had been born in Somalia, in 1983. When the fighting reached Mogadishu where they were living, their two older brothers went to live in the countryside with their mother. Mo, Hassan and their sister Ifrah went to live with their grandmother in the neighbouring country of Djibouti. Now Djibouti was caught up in the war, too. Mo and Hassan knew that their grandmother was growing increasingly worried about their safety.

That evening, their grandmother waited until they had all finished their meal before she turned to her grandchildren.

"Your father has been in touch," she said. The children's father had been born and brought up in London, and had gone back there to look for work. "He has found a job at last," their grandmother continued, "and has asked for three of his children to join him. It is safe in London and you will have a chance of a better life. Your father suggests that your older brothers, Liban and Omar, should both go, together with one of the twins."

Mo and Hassan stared at each other, scarcely able to take in their grandmother's dreadful news. Of course the war was bad — everybody in Djibouti and Somalia knew people who had been killed or injured in the fighting. But to split them up? They were twin brothers! They were the best of friends!

London would definitely be safer for the children. They knew if that was what their father had decided, then there could be no argument.

The big question was, which one of them would be going to London — Mo or Hassan?

Dusk was falling as the big black taxi drew up outside Mo and Hassan's grandmother's house. Mo had been the one chosen to go to the UK. Hassan was told he would follow on afterwards.

Now the taxi was waiting to take Mo
to the station to catch the train for
Addis Ababa in neighbouring Ethiopia.
There, another taxi would take him to
the airport and the flight to London.
Mo fought back the tears. It wasn't the
anxiety of going to live in a strange
country that upset him. It was the
thought that he would be leaving his
twin brother Hassan behind.

Mo's grandmother hugged him tight. "Be strong, Mohamed," she whispered. "Hassan will join you in London soon, I'm sure." Deep down, Mo wondered if that would ever really happen or whether his grandmother was saying it to try and make the parting just a little bit easier.

Mo got into the back of a taxi, then turned and waved to his grandmother, sister and twin brother. With a screech of tyres, the taxi pulled away into the deep darkness of the East African night.

Chapter Three:
Fight!

Mo sat on his own at the front of a classroom at a school in London. The teacher clapped her hands for silence.

"We have a new boy in class this morning," she announced. "Say hello to Mohamed, everyone!"

"Hello Mohamed!" the class chorused. Out of the corner of his eye, Mo saw that one hard-looking boy had not joined in with the others, but sat, his chair tilted back, with a big sneer on his face.

At break time, some of the other children in the class came up to talk to Mo. He didn't understand what they were saying. He had only learnt three phrases of English: "Excuse me," "Where is the toilet?" and "C'mon then".

The hard-looking boy who had been sneering in class approached Mo. He was still sneering. He muttered something under his breath. It didn't sound very pleasant. Mo decided he

had to say something to him. He chose
one of the English phrases he'd learnt,
though he wasn't sure what it meant.

"C'mon then."

The other boy clenched his fists. "Yeah? Right, you're on!" He gave Mo a shove. Mo shoved him back. Then the boy walloped Mo with his fist. Mo realised this wasn't like the play fighting he had done at home with his brother. He hit the boy back and soon the two of them were thumping each other hard.

"Fight! Fight!" chorused the boys in the playground.

Two teachers raced out of the school. One grabbed Mo and one got hold of the other boy. Then the teachers marched both boys off to the headteacher's office.

When Mo got back to class, he couldn't help but notice the admiring glances from the rest of the children. The new boy in school had taken on the class bully and had given him as good as he'd got.

Chapter Four:

Born To Run

Mo didn't find school life very easy. By the time he went to secondary school, he had a reputation for being a cheeky mischief-maker whose English wasn't up to much.

The first proper PE lesson Mo's class had was throwing the javelin. The PE teacher, whose name was Mr Watkinson, lined everybody up for a safety talk. When Mr Watkinson looked up at the end of his talk, he saw to his amazement that one boy in the class hadn't been listening to him at all. In fact, he was swinging from the nearby goalposts, paying no attention at all.

Mr Watkinson called him over.

"What's your name?" he asked the boy.

"Mo, sir."

Mo got a telling off and was sent to the back of the line. As a punishment, he would be the very last person in the class to have a go at throwing a javelin.

When at last it came to Mo's turn, he threw the javelin further than anyone else in the class. Mr Watkinson watched

in amazement as Mo went back to his place at the end of the line. He noticed how long the boy's stride was and suddenly realised that Mo was a natural athlete.

When the rest of the class went in to get changed, Mr Watkinson called Mo over.

"That was some throw you managed there, Mo," he said. "Have you ever thought about taking up athletics after school?"

Mo shrugged. "No," he replied.

"Do you like athletics?" asked Mr Watkinson.

"No."

"What do you like then?"

"Football."

"OK," said Mr Watkinson, "here's the deal. I'll let you have a half an hour kick around on the all-weather pitch after school. In return, you do half an hour cross-country training. What do you think?"

Mo grinned. "All right," he replied.

The deal worked. Mo turned up for cross-country training after school just so he could play football.

Mo took part in his first ever schools cross-country race in 1995, when he was twelve and in Year Seven. It was almost a total disaster. He didn't know the route and started off going in the wrong direction. He ended up having to follow the other kids so that he didn't get lost. Despite that he still managed to finish second.

Mr Watkinson congratulated Mo after the race. "You did well, Mo," he said. "So well that I've entered you for the County Championships cross-country race in a month's time."

Mo came fourth in that race, even though he had no proper running shoes.

In 1996, when Mo was 13, Mr Watkinson entered him for the English Schools cross-country competition. He came ninth.

"Mo," Mr Watkinson told him, "you're a natural athlete. You were born to run. I reckon one day you could compete for Britain."

"I don't want to be a runner," said Mo.

"What do you want to do, then?" sighed Mr Watkinson.

"I want to play football for Arsenal," replied Mo, with a smile.

Mr Watkinson smiled back. "I'll tell you what," he said. "If you win the English Schools cross-country competition next year, I'll buy you an Arsenal shirt. How about it?"

"OK," said Mo.

"Great," replied Mr Watkinson. "You've got the talent, but talent on its own isn't enough. You've got to put in the effort as well. That means training hard and running throughout the year."

Mr Watkinson said that Mo should join an athletics club, so that he could train and run at weekends and during the holidays.

The following year, the hard work and commitment paid off. Mo won the English Schools cross-country competition and Mr Watkinson bought him an Arsenal shirt.

In fact, Mo went on to win the English Schools cross-country championship five years in a row and although Mr Watkinson didn't buy Mo any more Arsenal shirts, he did drive the young athlete to training each week.

When he was 16, Mo was invited to go to a summer camp in Florida especially for young athletes who were seen as having the potential to become Olympians.

Chapter Five:

Eat, Sleep, Train

Mo still lived with his father in West London, though he often thought about the rest of his family back in Somalia, especially his twin brother Hassan.

Once he'd left school, Mo worked in a
fast food restaurant and a sports shop.
During his spare time he trained and ran
with Hounslow Athletics Club. To make

real progress as an athlete, he needed to take advantage of their top training facilities at Twickenham, but there was no way he could get there without a car — Mo couldn't drive. Driving lessons were expensive and there was no way he could afford them.

Luckily for Mo, the women's marathon world record holder, Paula Radcliffe, had been following his progress as a young distance runner. When she heard about Mo's plight she offered to pay for driving lessons for him.

Once he was able to use top training facilities, Mo quickly became a very successful junior athlete. In 2001 he won the European Junior 5,000 metres and cross-country titles. He was enjoying life. He had lots of friends and liked nothing more than going out clubbing until the early hours and sleeping in past 11 o'clock or so the next morning.

One day, Mo's agent, Ricky Simms, called him into his office. "How's it going then, Mo?" he asked.

Mo yawned. He'd had another late night. "Yeah... OK... Good."

"You may think it's 'good'," replied Ricky. "I think it's not good enough."

"Not good enough?" exclaimed Mo. "I'm Britain's top distance runner!"

"And are you going to leave it at that, or do you want to become the world number one?"

"Of course I do!"

Ricky looked hard at Mo. "Then you've got to sort yourself out," he said.

"What do you mean?" asked Mo with a frown.

"For a start, you've got to change
your lifestyle. Late nights are out.
If you're going to be a world-class
athlete you must have only one focus —
getting yourself into tip-top condition.
There's a group of world-class East
African runners staying in London at
the moment for the European circuit.
I recommend you go and see how they
live and train."

A couple of weeks later, Mo called in to Ricky Simms' office.

"I went to see those East African runners," he said.

"And..?" enquired Ricky.

"It's incredible," Mo told him. "These guys go to bed at nine and get up at six! They train in the morning, come back, eat, sleep, and then do some more training."

"So now you know that, what do you plan to do about it?" asked Ricky.

"There's a spare room in their house," replied Mo. "I'm moving in with them next week."

Chapter Six:

World Beater

Mo did well with his new regime.
Now he needed to prepare for the
biggest and most exciting challenge
of his career so far: the 2008 Beijing
Olympics. In 2006 he won his first senior

medal — gold in the European Cross-Country Championships. The following year, he came sixth in the World Championships.

Next Mo took a break from his preparations for the Olympics to visit his family in Somalia, which included seeing his twin brother Hassan. This was the first time the twins had seen each other since they were eight years old.

In 2008, Mo ran the fastest UK men's 10,000 metres time for almost eight years.

Mo's prospects for the 2008 Beijing Olympics were looking very good. By the time it came to the long distance running events, the rest of Team GB were doing well, too. They had won cycling and swimming golds. All eyes were now on Mo, the European Cross-Country gold medal holder. The newspapers had been full of stories about his chances in the 5,000 metres.

First of all though, Mo had to get through the qualifying stage — the heats. There were three heats. Mo was in heat two. The fastest four runners in his heat would go on through to the final. Mo wasn't overly worried. He knew he'd run faster times than many of the athletes out there on the track with him.

But as soon as he kicked off, Mo knew there was something wrong. He just didn't seem to have the rhythm to run the kind of race he knew he was capable of running. He finished sixth, not even making the cut for the finals.

Mo had never been more disappointed in his life. He felt he had let himself down, as well as his family and everyone who had been watching the race back in the UK and in Somalia.

Somehow though, he had to pick himself up and start preparing for the next Olympics: London 2012.

Chapter Seven:

Olympic Champion

During the build-up to 2012, Mo trained hard and ran well. He won gold at the 2010 European Championships and then again at the 2011 World Championships.

He had established himself as a world-class distance runner.

For London 2012, Mo was entered in not one, but two distance races: the 10,000 metres and the 5,000 metres. There were no preliminary heats for

the 10,000 metres though, just the final race. Mo couldn't help feeling relieved about this. He still had vivid and painful memories of the way he had crashed out in the 5,000-metres heats of the Beijing Olympics four years earlier.

Britain, and the whole of Somalia, waited in breathless expectation. The noise in the packed 80,000-capacity Olympic stadium was deafening. To win, Mo had to beat the greatest distance runner the world had ever seen, the Ethiopian Kenenisa Bekele. Could he do it?

With one lap to go, Mo was lying back in the field, but then, the crowd roaring him on, he kicked past Kenenisa Bekele to claim victory with a sprint finish. This was Great Britain's first ever 10,000 metres gold medal.

The crowd went wild with delight, as

did millions of people watching on television, including Mo's twin brother Hassan and his family, back in Somalia.

Less than three weeks later, Mo did it all again in the 5,000 metres final. He took the lead with 700 metres to go and crossed the finishing line with his arms outstretched, his eyes wide open with absolute joy.

There was just one more thing he had to do on this greatest of Olympic nights. Mo turned towards the crowd, where his wife and daughter, his old PE teacher Mr Watkinson and Paula Radcliffe were all sitting and began to do his now famous "Mobot" celebration dance.

And Mo had plenty to celebrate — he'd just become the UK's greatest ever distance runner.

Fact file
Mo Farah

Full name: Mohamed Farah

Nationality: British

Born: 23 March 1983, Mogadishu, Somalia

Height: 1.75 metres

Major Medals

- **2001 European Junior Championships**
  Gold, 5,000 metres
  Gold, Cross-Country

- **2006 European Cross-Country Championships**
  Gold

- **2010 European Championships**
  Gold, 5,000 metres
  Gold, 10,000 metres

- **2011 World Championships**
  Gold, 5,000 metres
  Silver, 10,000 metres

- **2012 Olympic Games**
  Gold, 10,000 metres
  Gold, 5,000 metres

Other Achievements and Honours

- 2011 and 2012 European Athlete of the Year
- 2013 Created a Commander of the (Order of the) British Empire (CBE)

The Mo Farah Foundation

The Mo Farah Foundation provides life-saving aid to some of the millions of people facing starvation and disease in East Africa. To find out more visit:

www.mofarahfoundation.org.uk

Bradley Wiggins

Bradley and his mum watched as the two riders sped round the cycle track. One bike stood out — it looked like something from a sci-fi movie. The rider's helmet was weird, too. It had a long point at the back going all the way down his neck. But the cyclist on the sci-fi bike soon powered past reigning world champion, Jens Lehmann.

"And it's gold for Chris Boardman, and for Great Britain!" screamed the commentator.

While his mum leapt around the room, whooping with delight, Bradley sat there staring at the TV. He couldn't take his eyes off Chris Boardman and his amazing Lotus super machine.

Bradley Wiggins was twelve years old, and he was hooked on bikes...

**Continue reading this story in:
DREAM TO WIN:
Bradley Wiggins**